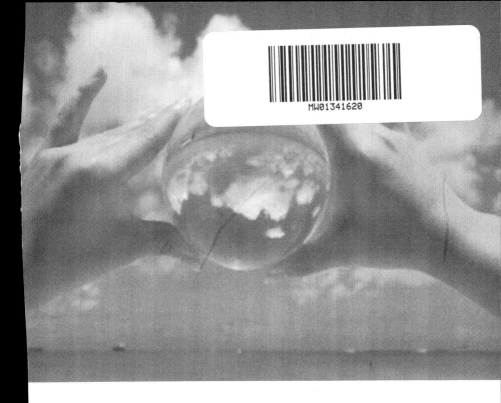

CLARITY

A revolutionary new approach to create organizational connectedness through shared clarity.

By Richard Yeager, Bruce Moorhouse and Jeffrey Meskill

This book is dedicated to the many people who have inspired and encouraged us throughout our lives and careers…

NOT THE ORDINARY BOOK

The stores are filled with books that contain theories of organizational excellence, growth, strategy, and leadership. We have read many of those books and have found them to be valuable.

This is not a book about theory. It is based on our real experiences of organizational life. We have seen, lived, and been impacted by these issues. The ideas and approaches discussed in this book come from our combined one hundred years at some of the world's finest companies and industries and through our work over almost two decades as senior consultants to more than thirty companies worldwide.

This book is also based on a simple reality. Organizations can compete in a number of ways such as product leadership, customer intimacy, or low cost, but there are no "new" or secret formulas for success or strategies. This makes the ability to execute paramount.

We wrote this book because we believe the degree to which an organization is "connected" to its formula for success is the number-one untapped execution opportunity in organizations today. Organizational connectedness is not possible without shared clarity. The impact of shared clarity is powerful and pervasive since it is part of the human spirit. It has significant performance benefits at all levels, from teams to small functional groups to the entire organization.

We wrote this book because we have learned that the great leaders create shared clarity—that great leaders view themselves as the "composer" of a clear formula for success that allows every member of the organization to fully understand the part they play in concert with others to help the organization achieve greatness together.

WHAT PEOPLE ARE SAYING

In writing this book we have interviewed and worked with hundreds of organizational leaders, each with many years of diverse organizational education and experience. They have repeatedly told us that this book provides unique perspectives and practical solutions around shared clarity that have never before been presented in such a thought-provoking or powerful way.

Clarity: First Edition

Copyright 2013 by Richard Yeager, Bruce Moorhouse, and Jeffrey Meskill

All rights reserved. No part of this book may be reproduced in any form whatsoever, by photography or xerography or by any other means, by broadcast transmission, by translation into any kind of language, nor by recording electronically or otherwise without permission in writing from the publisher, except by a reviewer, who may quote brief passages in critical article or reviews.

Editorial Assistance by Kimberlee Blair

Cover Photo: Masterfile Royalty Free

Printed in the United States of America

ISBN-10: 1480131628
ISBN-13: 9781480131620

Library of Congress Control Number: 2012919831
CreateSpace Independent Publishing Platform
North Charleston, South Carolina

TABLE OF CONTENTS

THE ELEPHANT IN THE ROOM..........................

THE PRINCIPLE OF SHARED CLARITY 2

INTRODUCTION 7

SECTION 1 - SHARED CLARITY BUSINESS CASE...... 21

SECTION 2 - CLARITY IN OUR LIVES 37

SECTION 3 - THE ANTIBODIES TO CLARITY.......... 45

SECTION 4 - THE BENEFITS OF SHARED CLARITY ... 67

SECTION 5 - CLARITY IS HUMAN 87

SECTION 6 - THE FUTURE IS NOW.................... 105

SECTION 7 - LEADING THE CONNECTED ORGANIZATION 113

SECTION 8 - BUILDING THE CONNECTED ORGANIZATION 127

OUR WORK 145

SUMMARY 147

ABOUT THE AUTHORS 151

**FINALLY, A BOOK
BASED ON A SIMPLE TRUTH:
CONNECTED ORGANIZATIONS
OUTPERFORM!**

CLARITY

*A revolutionary new approach to creating organizational
connectedness through shared clarity*

By Richard Yeager, Bruce Moorhouse, and Jeffrey Meskill

CLARITY

The Elephant in the Room

There is an elephant in the room in every organization.
Everyone knows he's there, but nobody talks about him.
We were never introduced to him.

Nobody ever taught us how to care for him.
The elephant gets in the way—he's a big distraction.
He sits in our meetings.
He impacts our decisions.
He takes up a lot of room.
He separates us.

He eats our food.
He drinks our water.
We have to take him outside regularly.
We have to walk him.
He wastes our time and our energy.

He attracts a lot of flies.
He swats them with his tail.
We are constantly ducking our heads.
We have to bathe him and dry him.
He sprays us with cold water.

He really smells.
He keeps growing.
He makes us meet more often.

We worry that he is going to roll over on top of us.
We think he might step on us.
He makes us anxious.
He makes us feel confused.
He makes us afraid.

He makes us uncertain.
He makes us feel unimportant.
He slows us down.
He is a downer.

Why aren't we talking about him?
Why don't we see him?
Who let him in the room?
Why was he let in room?
Who can help us get him out of here?
When will he leave?

CLARITY

THE PRINCIPLE OF SHARED CLARITY

The elephant in the room causes the frustration we feel when we don't know where we are going and how we'll get there.

The elephant is the lack of clarity—clarity that should be shared by everyone in the organization. This book is about the **Principle of Shared Clarity** and how to achieve it.

This book is about seeing the elephant and getting him out of the room.

The principle of shared clarity is simple, yet powerful...

The Principle of Shared Clarity states that:

Organizations Connected through Shared Clarity Outperform.

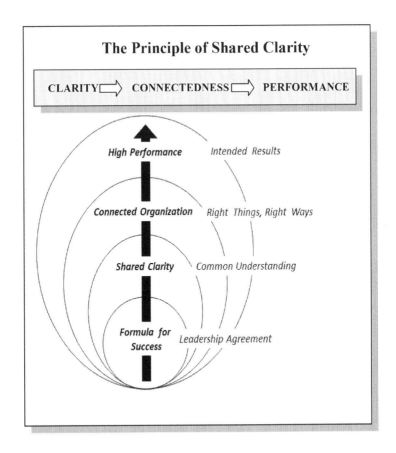

WHO WILL BENEFIT FROM THIS BOOK?

The benefits of the shared clarity principle are available to every part of the organization, from individual employees and leaders, to small functional groups or teams, to departments, to business units, to the total company or entity.

This book is intended for anyone who:

Is in, or aspires to be in, a leadership or managerial role in any type of organization.

Teaches, coaches, or mentors existing or aspiring organizational leaders or managers.

Is looking for ways to be better connected to their organization and who wants to use their human capabilities to feel valued and to make a difference.

INTRODUCTION

In today's world, the connectedness of the organization has never been more important. Through shared clarity, each organization creates a series of connections that provide performance benefits at all levels.

As the number one untapped execution issue today, the degree to which an organization is "connected" to its formula for success remains an essential part to being successful. However, overall connectedness is impossible without a common understanding of exactly what success is and how it will be measured and achieved.

This book is about the benefits of shared clarity to people and to the organization. The need for shared clarity is not limited by the authority of one's position. Instead, creating shared clarity must be embedded in the very fabric of the organization. It must extend to every function and to every person. This means that everyone in the organization, regardless of their role or position, must understand the importance of shared clarity and must be a catalyst to achieving it.

The benefits of shared clarity can be significant. We have found a short, *One Minute Shared Clarity Test* can help determine the degree of benefit that shared clarity can have for an organization.

The One Minute Shared Clarity Test

Question#1: To what degree are the actions and decisions of your organization's people responsible for its success?

Question #2: How important is it that each person in your organization understands how they can contribute to success?

Question #3: Does everyone in your organization clearly understand how they can contribute to success?

Question # 4: How do you know that shared clarity exists?

Introduction

THE CONNECTED ORGANIZATION - What is it?

Webster's Dictionary defines "connected" as "something that is coherently united, joined or linked."

In writing this book, we chose the term "Connected Organization" because our experience has shown that this same definition applies to high-performing organizations. Great organizations find ways to have everyone feel and act "connected" to the organization's formula for success and to one another.

As we observed high performing, connected organizations, we realized that none of this could be accomplished without the PRINCIPLE OF SHARED CLARITY. Without the common understanding achieved through shared clarity, how can any organization operate coherently in a united, joined, or linked way?

We also realized that shared clarity is elusive because it must be achieved in organizations made up of real people, each with his or her unique experiences, perceptions, and emotions. Because of this, it is much easier to talk about clarity in a general sense than to actually create clarity that is "personalized" in each person's heart and mind.

From our experiences, we also have concluded that when it comes to creating shared clarity, organizational leaders face a personal challenge and an enigma. Why not just create a partially united, joined, or linked organization by telling everyone in the organization what to do and how to do it, when they need to know it? This may often seem much easier.

It's a natural instinct of many leaders to believe that the organization is best served if they tell everyone what to do as a "conductor". This is natural because leaders often have a unique "tops-down" perspective. Unfortunately, playing only the more natural role of conductor without first composing and communicating a common "musical score" jeopardizes organizational connectedness.

Not focusing on creating shared clarity is also a natural consequence of the comfort that comes from leaders wearing only the conductor hat. This one-hat vs. two-hat issue was illustrated by one CEO (who was obviously more comfortable as a conductor) when he told us, "You know, they all report to me. I can tell them what to do."

The leadership instinct to conduct vs. compose also creates blind spots when it comes to creating shared clarity. This becomes evident when we talk to leaders about creating a connected organization through shared clarity and they tell us, "I see where that might be a problem somewhere else, but everything's pretty clear from here."

The blind spot is only revealed when we ask them a few simple questions…

Do you think organizational connectedness through shared clarity is more practical or emotional? Is the goal for your people to feel connected, be connected, or act connected? Or is it all of these?

Introduction

Could you tell us about the specific information you use to create shared clarity? This could include information around your organization's definition and formula for success, your goals, etc. Where does this information come from, and how do you use it?

How effective has your communication been? What have you written down and communicated to help everyone in the organization truly and personally understand the full story of the organization's success formula today and in the future? If you asked the same employee or groups of employees about this, what would they say?

Can your employees translate what they do to your organization's formula for success? If we picked an employee or group of employees at random and asked them how their work and how they performed it was related to the organization's formula for success, could they tell us? Would they all say the same thing? Have you asked them?

Do you think the level of shared clarity can be measured in a quantifiable way? If so, do you measure it? What do the results tell you? Is organizational connectedness measured from the tops down or from the bottoms up?

Introduction

THE FORMULA FOR SUCCESS

We have talked to many people, from front-line employees to senior executives, about the idea of shared clarity and the connected organization. In the beginning we characterized our work around what we called "strategic clarity."

After a while, it became obvious that the word "strategic" had a lot of negative baggage associated with it. The average employee would tell us, "I'm not responsible for the strategy," while senior executives would tell us the word "strategy" conjured up images of some secretive, future-oriented plan known only by a few top people.

All of this has taught us that people in organizations relate best to what they do and what they see <u>today</u>.

Since then, we have used the term "Formula for Success" because we find it to be far more relevant to the entire organization.

The formula for success resonates with people. People intuitively understand it and identify with it. They are better able to see how they connect to it. We find that when people understand the formula for success, they adapt the things they do, how they do them, and the results they achieve to the organization's intended outcomes.

The challenge is to create shared understanding around a formula for success that is properly and completely defined.

CLARITY

In approaching this challenge, we find that too much emphasis is often placed on finding and creating a "perfect" formula for success. *We believe shared clarity is far more important than the futile search for perfection of the strategy.* We're sure we all know of many great companies and organizations that have not fundamentally changed their formula for success for many years. Instead, they have excelled by remaining connected to it.

For people to understand it, the formula for success, even if not "perfect," must be clear to them as individuals and to everyone in the organization.

In our view, the ingredients to creating shared clarity around the formula for success are found in the answers to a number of key questions. These questions must first be asked and then must be answered in a sufficient level of detail to make sure that leadership agreement truly exists and to achieve shared understanding across the entire organization. The answers to these questions are the "raw material" for shared clarity.

What is success? What is our purpose? What do we want to be? What differentiates us? What capabilities do we need? What are our priorities? What are our goals, and how will we achieve them? How will we measure success? How will we operate?

Introduction

SHARED CLARITY

The principle of shared clarity applies everywhere – to organizations and teams of all sizes and types and to us as people and to our personal relationships.

Every organization has a formula for success, regardless of whether it is implicitly or explicitly defined. Every organization also has customers (sometimes internal ones), products or services (also sometimes internal ones), financial resources, technology, and people.

Unfortunately, clarity about the formula for success cannot be shared if it doesn't exist in the first place. It's obvious that if the leadership team is not on the same page, it's not possible to expect others to be uniformly clear. It's also obvious that if different communicators send clear but conflicting messages, shared clarity cannot exist.

For shared clarity to occur, the organization's formula for success must provide a level and type of clarity that is unique to the individuals or groups in the organization. Each part, person, and function of the organization, when viewing the formula for success, must be able to "connect" what they do with it.

For this connection to happen, the organization's formula for success must create common understanding around the answers to certain key questions. These are the questions that are natural for the functional people within the organization to ask, but that often go unanswered.

What defines our success? What is our customer value proposition, and how do we deliver it? What products and services should we develop, and what are the characteristics they should have? How and where should we employ our technology? What types of skills and capabilities should we hire or develop?

In the final analysis, an organization's performance comes from the functional actions and decisions of its people. This makes the interpretation and understanding of the answers to these questions very important. If the answers are interpreted differently by people or by the various parts of the organization, performance will suffer.

All of this boils down to a key principle: the formula for success (even if not perfect) must be clearly and completely defined. It must be then be communicated in sufficient detail so that all parts of the organization and all people in it can find the right "hooks" that help them guide their specific actions and decisions to the right things, right ways, and right results.

SHARED CLARITY: From Concept to Process

Shared clarity is not about goodness, it's about results.

We believe developing shared clarity is just like any other process that takes place within an organization. It's really no different from processes like customer service, marketing, or sales. Unfortunately, as a process, shared clarity is often "in the shadows" and not managed or even recognized as a process by many organizational leaders.

Because it is a process, shared clarity can be designed, managed, and improved, but it must be approached in a systematic way. Like any other process, its ongoing success depends on both asking the right questions and the degree of consensus within the answers.

To approach shared clarity as a process and in a logical and holistic way, we have developed and use what we call the "Shared Clarity Map."

Introduction

Shared Clarity Map

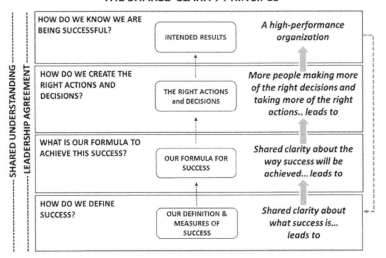

The Shared Clarity Map embodies the shared clarity principle: in organizations connected through shared clarity, more people will do more of the right things, in the right ways, to produce the intended results.

The Shared Clarity Map provides the framework for key shared clarity questions that must be addressed and illustrates the cause-and-effect relationships between them.

Shared Clarity Map (with key clarity questions)

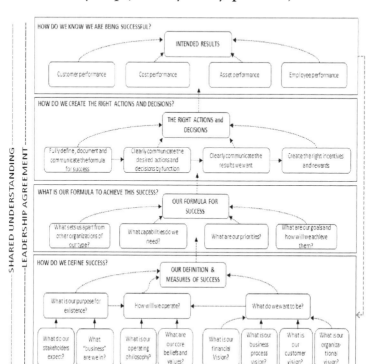

Since shared clarity is a constantly changing target, the Shared Clarity Map also provides a reusable, process-oriented foundation for the on-going development and measurement shared clarity.

The rest of this book is dedicated to the challenge of achieving shared clarity.

Section 1
Shared Clarity:
The Business Case

This section of the book provides a summary of why and how shared clarity adds value to the organization.

The Opportunity

The business case for shared clarity is logical and clear. Even a small investment in the creation of shared clarity yields significant returns in the form of greatly improved organizational performance and vastly reduces business and operational risk.

We wrote this book because we believe in the potential of shared clarity. We've seen how great organizations use shared clarity to excel and outperform.

We also wrote this book because we know that the potential of shared clarity has not been realized in many organizations and we've seen the devastating impact that a lack of shared clarity can have.

Our lens is our combined experiences from both the outside and the inside. From the outside, for more than sixteen years we have worked as senior consultants to more than three dozen companies and hundreds of executives worldwide. From the inside, we have seen and lived these issues through our almost one hundred years of firsthand experience working with some of the world's finest companies, and in mega-industries like professional services, global products and services, and innovation. We've also seen the impacts as consumers and customers.

We've seen the reality of more than thirty years of research that says aligned and integrated organizations outperform their nearest competitors by every major financial measure.

We've seen example after example of the organizational effectiveness and efficiencies that result from the connected organization and how these are a significant competitive and strategic advantage. We've confirmed what the research has shown time and time again: connected organizations enjoy greater customer and employee satisfaction and loyalty, and produce superior returns to shareholders.

Our work has confirmed the validity of a groundbreaking *Harvard Business Review* study that found that more than one-third of a disconnected organization's potential is wasted due to shared clarity-related factors.

We wrote this book because we believe that connectedness through shared clarity is the ultimate destination for great people, great organizations, and great leaders.

· · ·

The Evidence

We also wrote this book because we were frustrated. One hundred years working in and with corporate America can do that to you!

We are frustrated because when we talk to people within an organization about shared clarity, our message almost always resonates as true. They quickly give us many examples of how they feel disconnected, and they quickly recite war stories of the disconnectedness they see in their organizations on a daily basis.

On the other hand, when we talk to organizational leaders, we often come away with the impression that the evidence of the lack of shared clarity we present seems to apply everywhere but to their organization.

We wondered: How could such extensive and overwhelming external evidence of organizational disconnectedness as shown below be valid if shared clarity exists?

"We surveyed hundreds of executives at western multi-nationals in emerging markets, and more than a third either couldn't identify strongly with a clear strategy or didn't understand their role in the strategy." Michael Griffin,

Executive Director, Corporate Executive Board; *CFO Magazine*, November, 2011

CLARITY

"A mere 7% of employees today fully understand their company's business strategies and what's expected of them to help achieve company goals." Robert S. Kaplan and David P. Norton, *The Strategy-Focused Organization*.

Therefore, we decided to focus this book on solutions—solutions that address the overwhelming evidence that the principle of SHARED CLARITY is the untapped key to human and organizational connectedness and success.

• • •

The "Hard Wire"

We know there is a direct correlation (a "hard wire") between shared clarity and organizational performance. Most people we talk to will readily acknowledge this is true.

While this connection clearly exists, our experiences have taught us the challenges of "connecting the soft stuff with the hard stuff." As Michael Hammer once said, "The soft stuff is the hard stuff."

We've found that it is easier and more natural for most organizational leaders to understand and manage "hard facts" like sales numbers, volumes, employee counts, margins, and profit. In fact, we have seen (and participated in) sessions that were supposed to focus on the future strategy only to have them quickly change to a discussion of last quarter's "numbers."

To some degree this "reactive thinking" is normal. It's natural to first recognize and address the impact of the past when it is presented in the form of current results. And while these current results can't be changed, it's certainly a valuable management exercise to understand why today's results are what they are.

On the other hand, we've found it is much more difficult for leaders and managers to connect today's events, decisions, and actions to future results.

This requires "forward thinking." The "if, then" approach that forward thinking entails may appear counterintuitive. And as some of our clients have told us, when we try to create a "hard-wire connection" in our minds between the soft activities and decisions of today and tomorrow's hard result, "It makes our heads hurt."

The need for forward thinking is another reason we will use the term "formula for success." We believe the term "formula for success" better embodies that fact that there is a "hard wire" cause-and-effect relationship between every action and decision in the organization today and future organizational performance. It also better defines and more clearly communicates to everyone in the organization what is required by them today in terms of the doing the right things in the right ways and getting the right results.

. . .

Performance Gained

The correlation between shared clarity, connectedness, and organizational performance is direct and real. Unfortunately, this connection is often out of the direct sight of management and leadership.

This is because the manifestation of connectedness (or lack of connectedness) to the organization's formula for success is often subtle and "below the surface." It plays out in the hundreds of actions and decisions made every day by everyone up and down and across the organization. Even though the evidence of connectedness (or lack thereof) may be hard to see, its impacts are significant and have a cumulative effect on the organization's performance.

In disconnected organizations, the roots of the lost performance that shows up today were often planted long ago. One has to only think about the key drivers of organizational performance to realize how they are impacted (positively or negatively) by organizational connectedness or the lack thereof. Day-to-day operations, sales and marketing, product/service development, customer contact and relationships, resource deployment decisions, projects and programs, employee training and development, external public relations, and internal communications are but a few of the areas directly impacted by the degree of shared clarity.

Because the formal "reach" of leaders is limited, connecting the organization around a clearly understood formula for success

CLARITY

is the "invisible hand" that guides the many important activities that take place beyond the leader's line of sight.

As such, shared clarity creates a natural, yet powerful connecting mechanism that also frees the leader from spending time on firefights, intra-organization coordination and on strategically unimportant minutia.

Because there is less confusion, variability, and ad-hoc-ism, a connected organization exponentially magnifies the leader's influence and impact and allows time for the leader to truly lead.

• • •

What is Shared Clarity?

A law of human nature is that what's clear to one person may not be clear to another person. We all have seen cases where two people see exactly the same thing and interpret it very differently.

We have found that this is the same issue many organizations face in trying to connect the organization around their formula for success.

For instance, mission and vision statements are often elegantly worded and inspiring. Unfortunately, we have found that they do not provide the level of clarity needed for each and every person to figure out what they mean to them.

For example, a typical statement we have seen is something like: "We are customer focused in everything we do." While employees see this statement on the walls, in internal communications, and on the organization's website, they are asking themselves: Exactly what should I do or not do? How should I do it? What are the results I am aiming for?

As a real example, we have found that personalized clarity around a customer-focused mission statement like this one can be greatly increased by simply communicating something like the following:

"We use technology to personalize service, not de-personalize it."

"Our customers—internal and external—are our friends."

"Our vision has nothing to do with pushing products. It's about building lifelong relationships with our customers."

"We want to offer products and services to our customers that save them time and money."

This simple example shows how making one aspect of the formula for success more specific (and clear) allows it to be properly translated by more people in the organization to what they do, how they do it, and to the decision they make.

In summary, shared clarity cannot be subject to multiple interpretations. It must define both the right and wrong choices. It must be communicated in ways that allow every employee to understand and personalize it specific his or her role in the organization.

· · ·

The Value

The business case for the connected organization is absolute. **Connected Organizations Outperform. Period!**

We have seen that Connected Organizations:

- ✔ Create trust, a critical commodity, which is rarer today than ever.

- ✔ Significantly reduce operational risk where the consequences are greater than ever.

- ✔ Help their people feel they are "connected" in spite of changing human perceptions and expectations in today's complicated world.

- ✔ Provide more value to their customers, who have greater power and choice than ever before.

- ✔ Prevent critical missteps at all levels of the organization, which in today's networked world can quickly be elevated to the "risk the business" level.

- ✔ Provide needed relief from the "clutter" of today's business environment, where time and attention are scarce resources.

- ✔ Focus everyone on the right things, right ways, and right results implied by the organization's formula for success.

The Numbers

Shared clarity is not about "goodness." It's about results.

We like to say that the power of connected organizations comes from them using shared clarity to "connect the <u>business side</u> to the <u>people side</u> to the <u>bottom line</u>."

Numerous studies, including a landmark *Harvard Business Review* study on organizational performance, have shown that, on average, organizations operate at 40 percent or less of possible shared clarity, and as a result, waste about 37 percent of their potential. Therefore, the impacts of improvements in organizational connectivity are significant, as summarized in the table below.

• • •

CLARITY

Connected Organization Index (COI)	Customer Satisfaction	Customer Turnover Rate	Cost/Unit	Employee Satisfaction	Employee Turnover Rate	Gross Margin	Return on Sales	ROI	OVERALL CHANGE IN PERFORMANCE
9.0 - 10.0	+30%	-20%	-30%	+50%	-10%	+15%	+25%	+15%	+35%
8.0 - 8.9	+25%	-16%	-25%	+40%	-8%	+12%	+20%	+12%	+25%
7.0 - 7.9	+20%	-12%	-20%	+30%	-6%	+9%	+15%	+9%	+15%
6.0 - 6.9	+15%	-8%	-15%	+20%	-4%	+6%	+10%	+6%	+10%
5.0 - 5.9	+10%	-4%	-10%	+10%	-2%	+3%	+5%	+3%	+5%
4.0 - 4.9	TYPICAL ORGANIZATION TODAY								
3.0 - 3.9	-10%	+4%	+5%	+10%	+2%	-3%	-5%	-3%	-5%
2.0 - 2.9	-15%	+8%	+10%	+20%	+4%	-6%	-10%	-6%	-10%
< 2.0	-20%	+12%	+15%	+30%	+6%	-9%	-15%	-9%	-15%

Why do connected organizations have better results? The answer is intuitively obvious: organizations that are well connected through shared clarity will simply make more of the right decisions and take more of the right actions (and avoid more of the wrong ones).

Therefore, as shown in the above table, even small gains in shared clarity (as measured by the Connected Organization Index—COI) will yield significant improvements in customer, cost, employee, and profitability performance.

Section 2
Clarity in Our Lives

Clarity in our lives is a powerful force.

This section of the book provides a series of examples and stories drawn from our corporate and consulting experiences. We believe these help illustrate the key dimensions of clarity and the challenges of creating the shared clarity needed for a connected organization.

The Power of Clarity in Our Lives

Bruce teaches at the University of Minnesota.

Near the end of the semester, the students are asked to make a short presentation in class and describe the life they want to make for themselves. Over the years, he has found that they always try to answer four basic questions:

1. Where am I going?
2. What do I have to do to get there?
3. Where will my growth come from?
4. How will I know when I get there?

Watching these students think about these issues has taught us that these questions of clarity are the fundamental questions of life.

This has confirmed that the same search for clarity is relevant to the organization because it is fundamental to the human spirit.

• • •

The Power of Clarity in Our Work

Late every summer, the senior leadership team of the organization goes off on a "leadership retreat" to work on their strategic plan.

When they return to headquarters, someone is asked to develop a communiqué to send out to employees about the new plan. This person goes out and interviews the twenty or so leaders involved in the planning discussion and then creates a document to communicate "to the troops" where the organization is going.

The interesting thing is that, when interviewed, the leadership group never seems to agree on what they had talked about during those few days out of the office. Everybody has a different version of the decisions made.

We have both seen and lived this common phenomenon. It has caused us to ask ourselves: If twenty people sitting in the same room for three days can't agree on where they are going as an organization, how can hundreds or even thousands of employees spread around the world be expected to understand the direction in a unified way?

. . .

Am I Going Crazy?

Organizational life can make people think they are going crazy. People ask: Is there something wrong with me? What am I doing wrong? Why is this happening? This doesn't make sense. I feel disconnected. I feel powerless.

Sometimes things can look saner if we learn to become an observer from the outside of the organization. From this outside perspective, we are better able to see the roles that everybody is playing, and we can more clearly understand exactly what people are doing and why they are doing it.

We can better understand how organizational systems work. We can see how predictable people can be when they are assigned a role within the system.

It can all begin to make sense. We can see different and better ways to experience our power and our freedom, and to feel connected to the organization we are part of.

Developing these observation skills can help us see the overall organization more clearly, which is an essential ingredient to creating a more connected organization.

Seeing the system from the outside provides the clarity needed to change the system in a positive way.

• • •

Section 3
The Antibodies to Clarity

Antibody: *Part of the human immune system used to identify and neutralize the negative impacts of foreign objects.*

Antibodies to Clarity - Introduction

Shared clarity is almost like a foreign object. There are many factors that work against it. This section of the book explores the typical barriers (antibodies) shown below that stand in the way of the leadership agreement and common understanding that shared clarity requires.

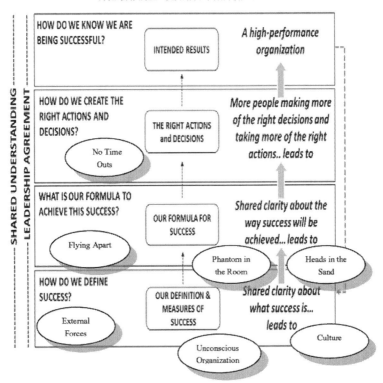

Clarity Antibody #1:
External Forces

More than ever, outside forces are challenging our ability to connect the organization. These forces influence us as individuals and the organization as a whole. These are the forces of new technologies, the instantaneousness and overload of information, social media, rapidly changing norms, and the pressures brought about by globalization.

The impact of these forces becomes quite evident when, as one of our clients told us, "My entire day is emptying my inbox. I don't really have time for much else."

These external forces distract us. They cloud the lens of clarity. They limit our ability to focus on the important things. They take away our time and attention. They beat us down and wear us out. They can even eat away at our willingness to deal the issue of shared clarity at all.

If not recognized, dealt with, and neutralized, these disruptive forces can make it difficult for the organization's formula for success to be commonly understood, communicated, and executed.

• • •

Clarity Antibody #2:
Flying Apart

As organizations grow and become more complex, they naturally begin to deconstruct or "fly apart." This can take various forms, such as decentralized operations, geographic dispersion, and the extensive use of contractors or out-sourcing.

Some business models, such as highly decentralized organizations or franchises, are based on the principle of deconstructed operations sometimes to the point of allowing separate ownership or management of parts of the deconstructed business.

It's quite natural for the "deconstructed" parties like contractors or franchisees to not have the same level of passion about the overall organization's formula for success or strategy, instead being more concerned about their own issues and successes.

The good news is that today's technology makes it easier to communicate and share critical information across and outside of organizational lines. On the other hand, technology is a natural catalyst for deconstruction because it makes it easier.

The bottom line is that as inevitable organizational deconstruction occurs, the challenge to create a connected organization through shared clarity becomes even greater.

For this reason, it is more important than ever that connectedness encompasses the organization's extended stakeholders like suppliers, outsource vendors, alliance partners, and even customers.

• • •

Clarity Antibody #3:
The Phantom

We often have asked ourselves: Could the absence of shared clarity be like a "phantom" whose presence and impact everyone in the organization sees, hears, and senses but at the same time seems oblivious to?

As evidence, many organizations have admitted to us they have the following:

- ✔ Our financial and human resources are not always directed at the right things.

- ✔ We don't always develop the specific skills and expertise we need.

- ✔ Our customer contacts and relationships don't create maximum value for our business.

- ✔ Our products and services don't produce maximum returns for our business.

- ✔ Our internal business processes are not optimized for our business.

- ✔ We don't always satisfy the needs and expectations of our key stakeholders.

✔ Our external image and reputation can be improved.

✔ Our people don't always produce maximum value for our business.

✔ Our organizational culture, beliefs, and core values don't fully support our formula for success.

If the lack of shared clarity is a root cause of these issues, why is so little attention paid to it by organizational leaders?

Is the phantom at work?

• • •

Clarity Antibody #4:
Heads in the Sand

As we said earlier, it is indisputable that the connectedness of the organization has a direct and traceable impact on business performance.

If organizational connectedness clearly leads to higher performance, then how then do we reconcile the following two facts?

As part of a continuing body of evidence, a landmark study by *Harvard Business Review* several years ago finds that almost 40 percent of organizational performance is lost due to clarity and alignment factors.

• • •

Less than 10 percent of employees and only 50 percent of executives clearly understand what the organization is trying to accomplish and their role in its success.

Why, if there is such an apparent correlation between low levels of clarity and losses in organization performance, are we not aware of a single organization anywhere that measures or benchmarks the degree of organizational connectedness to its formula for success in a consistent and holistic way?

• • •

Clarity Antibody #5:
No Time-Outs

One of the most significant antibodies to shared clarity is everyday pressures.

Unlike a football game, there are no time-outs in organizations. Every hour, every day, every week, every month, at all levels of the organization, employees take dozens, hundreds, or even thousands of actions and make important decisions that affect the organization's success or failure. Many of these actions and decisions are invisible to the organization's leaders.

In the absence of shared clarity, any movement toward or away from the organization's formula for success that results from these actions and decisions is not only hard for leaders to see, but also has a high probability of moving the organization in the wrong direction or at least sideways. Because there are no time outs, and the definition of value-added is unclear, low-value or even counterproductive work is also much more likely to exist and to be created.

With an absence of shared clarity, it's easy for the organization's leaders to believe, because they are continuing to control the organization's "rudder" by sending out orders and formulating policies and procedures, that everyone is executing the formula for success and doing so under full power. Unfortunately, without shared clarity, bad things (often unseen by leadership) will and do happen—every day.

Because there are no time-outs, it's up to organizational leaders to make sure that everyone in the organization has the clear understanding of the organization's formula for success they want and deserve. Only with this understanding can the organization's "engine room" be connected to the rudder. Only with shared clarity can the leader, as "the captain of the ship," make sure day-to-day actions and decisions fuel the "full speed ahead" necessary to achieve the organization's goals.

• • •

Clarity Antibody #6:
Culture

Because it is always at play in any organization, organizational culture is a powerful antibody to shared clarity.

Time and again we have seen leaders try unsuccessfully to implement changes that are foreign to the company's culture.

Take, for example, how the 3M culture of innovation and entrepreneurship that had sustained the company for a hundred years worked to actively resist any change to more standardization and centralization pushed by new company leadership. This is because, as a natural part of 3M's culture, each division had always been empowered to run its business with a clear focus on the marketplace. Empowerment, delegation, responsibility for results, and the freedom to innovate were prized and rewarded. The ideas of standardization and centralization were foreign to the 3M culture.

This example illustrates how the organization's culture can stand in the way of creating a connected organization. While at 3M the long-embedded culture helped to create and sustain the organization's connectedness, it made change difficult.

The key lesson is that when attempting to create a more connected organization, fundamental beliefs and behaviors must be taken seriously and must be managed as an integral and important part of the change process. Particularly important are the cultural norms around the role of leadership, accountability, empowerment, communication, and trust, since these are the pillars of the connected organization.

Executing a formula for success will always involve some degree of change. Creating a level of acceptance to the needed change within the culture is one of the most powerful tools to overcoming the cultural antibody to shared clarity.

• • •

Clarity Antibody #7:
The Unconscious Organization

Organizational life is complicated. Much of it is outside of our consciousness and can actually be invisible to us. For example, we can easily fail to see that how people behave in an organization is often a direct result of the role they see themselves playing.

For many years, we have done a simulation where we assign people to be senior leaders, middle managers, or low-level employees. The amazing thing is that depending on where people are assigned in the simulation, their behavior is quite predictable.

Within five minutes of starting the simulation, the employee group often begins to form a union. The senior management group quickly ignores the rest of the team and begins to work quite independently from the rest of the organization. The middle management group often looks around trying to figure out what to do. These are predictable behaviors. The leader's inability to recognize them is a barrier to shared clarity.

For instance, how many suggestions for significant business process improvements or new revenue-generating ideas might come from lower-level employees if they truly understand the organization's formula for success and if they think about their job through the eyes of a leader or middle manager or vice versa?

• • •

Clarity Antibody #8:
Seeing Only the Trees

One of our big problems around creating clarity in our organizational lives is that we are often unable to truly see the organization and the system that we work in. Instead of seeing the overall picture of how the organization works as a system, we see individual problems and individual personalities. We tend to the see the trees rather than the forest. This makes our explanations for the problems that we face and the solutions we create very personal. That is why it hurts so much when we perceive things aren't going well.

On the other hand, when we look at the organization as a system, we can "zoom out," and a completely new world opens up to us. When we understand that every system, from the simplest in nature to the most complex organization, engages in similar processes, we can begin to see the organization with a new sense of clarity.

Creating a connected organization requires the ability to look at the organization holistically as a system and to also recognize that it is a system made up of real people who have the innate desire to participate, to feel valued and to take pride in what they do.

• • •

The Antibodies to Clarity

Actions You Can Take Today

✔ Answer the questions on pages 53-54 on a scale of zero to five, with zero being never and five being always. Add up your score. Ask yourself if the lack of shared clarity might be at play.

✔ Perform the simulation described on page 61 and see what you learn.

✔ Evaluate whether or how your organization measures the degree of shared clarity today.

✔ Discuss the specific barriers to shared clarity in your organization with your peers.

Section 4
The Benefits of Shared Clarity

This section of the book explores the benefits of shared clarity and its significance to organizational performance.

The Benefits of Shared Clarity - Introduction

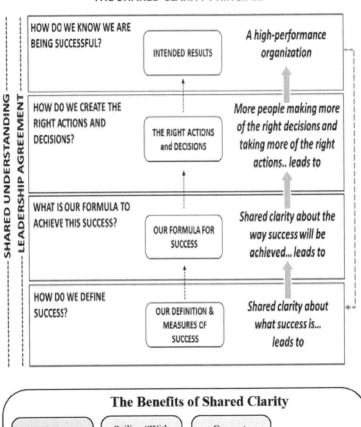

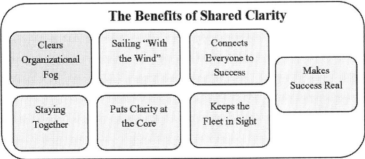

Shared Clarity Benefit #1:
Clears the Organizational Fog

Dateline: Marco Polo International Airport, Venice, Italy. "All flights are canceled due to fog."

Venice, Italy, is one of the world's foggiest cities. Each year, hundreds of flights are canceled or delayed, stranding thousands of passengers. Venice's fog is an act of nature, so little can be done except to wait for it to clear, but its impacts are profound: major inefficiencies in the basic purpose of transportation—getting people from point A to point B on time.

Just like the fog found in nature, most organizations operate in an "organizational fog." This fog is created by a lack of shared clarity around the organization's formula for success.

The impacts of organizational fog are much the same as the fog found in Venice. Because the direction and priorities are unclear across the entire organization, just like the planes in Venice, important initiatives are delayed or never take off at all.

Organizational fog hinders creating a connected organization because it shrouds the path to collective action and success. The members of the organization are forced to guess or interpret the path ahead and to take the actions they hope are consistent with that path.

CLARITY

And just like the dangers presented by a real fog, organizational fog greatly increases the risks of moving too slow, too fast, too far, or in the wrong direction.

• • •

Shared Clarity Benefit #2:
Sailing with the Wind

It is a well-known law of navigation that when a ship is adrift with no power, it will naturally turn into the wind and then slowly move backwards regardless of its intended destination.

Organizations are much the same.

The source of any organization's power comes from connecting the hearts and minds of its people to the right things. Shared clarity requires both understanding and acceptance. If all of the people, from leadership to front-line employees, do not share a common understanding of or commitment to the organization's formula for success, then just like a ship, the organization will turn against the wind and slowly drift away from its intended destination.

Unfortunately, evidence of the lack of connectedness in many organizations is found in numerous studies. For example, a study by Robert Kaplan and David Norton outlined in their landmark book *The Strategy-Focused Organization* showed that only about 7 percent of employees in American businesses understand their organization's strategy and their role in it. With these statistics, it's not surprising that the organization's members (the engine room crew) provide only limited power because they are unclear about specifically what they are supposed to do, how they are supposed to do it, and what results they are expected to achieve.

CLARITY

When there is shared clarity about what needs to be accomplished and why it's important, the connected organization is able to operate with "all hands on deck" and sail with the wind at full power toward its intended destination.

• • •

Shared Clarity Benefit #3:
Connects Everyone to Success

Like us, you have probably been aboard a flight where the flight plan by the pilots was flawlessly executed. You departed on time, gained altitude to avoid turbulence, heard from the pilot about the weather at your destination, and touched down with perfect precision—but you departed the plane thinking about what a bad experience that plane ride was.

The flight crew did great. It was the "stuff" the rest of the crew did that was the problem.

Passengers had to be directed from the back to the front because there was too much carry-on luggage, or you learned for the first time that you had to pay for a meal or even a certain seat. Or there was the time Jeff's daughter, then at age ten, did not receive any help stowing her suitcase because the flight attendant thought the suitcase was too large to fit (it wasn't).

What's going on here? It's pretty clear it was not the airline's intent to provide bad service. The crew members all seemed like nice people, but they seemed disconnected from the formula for success. Because the cabin crew seemed unable to understand and translate the goals of the overall organization to how they carried out their day-to-day jobs, a great flight was ruined for their customers.

CLARITY

These experiences capture the true promise of the connected organization—an organization where everyone, from top to bottom, side to side, and internally and externally, clearly understands the organization's formula for success, their specific role in it, and exactly what it means to their actions and decisions.

• • •

Shared Clarity Benefit #4:
Puts Clarity at the Core

The current and historical evidence is clear. Forty percent of all newly created companies last less than ten years. One-third of the companies listed on the 1970 Fortune 500 have vanished. The news is full of stories about companies who had great visions and well-thought-out strategies but seemed incapable of executing them well over time.

On the other hand, there are exceptions, like Stora, a Swedish pulp, paper, and chemical company that is seven hundred years old, and Sumitomo, a Japanese conglomerate that began in 1590.

Why do some companies grow and prosper while most of the others die?

Our experiences have led us to an inescapable conclusion and truth that we use with our clients: "Leaders are temporary, conditions change, but clarity endures."

We believe the ongoing ability to create shared clarity about the organization's formula for success and connect it to people's hearts and minds is the core ingredient for enduring greatness.

Few organizations can put claim to this precious resource.

• • •

Shared Clarity Benefit #5:
Staying Together

Business Start-Up CEO. "I can look every one of our people in the eye and tell them exactly what we are trying to do and why. That way I know everyone gets it and that we're all on the same page."

The steps to achieving shared clarity are difficult for all organizations, but the challenge becomes even greater as organizations grow and become more complex.

As organizations grow in size and complexity, creating a connected organization requires the leaders to ask themselves and others a different set of more "purpose centered" questions:

✔ How will we define and measure our success?

✔ What are our success formula's priorities and themes?

✔ What are our goals, and why are they important?

✔ What actions are needed, and who must take them?

✔ What we should engage our people around?

Answering these questions can often be easier and simpler in smaller organizations, where leaders are physically close to the people and the organization is relatively flat. As organizations grow, the face-to-face, personal contacts that worked well in the past just aren't possible anymore. It becomes more and more difficult to have everyone "stay together."

We believe shared clarity is the key to keeping organizations together. This is because shared clarity significantly extends and expands the leader's influence to areas where he or she can no longer "reach" as the organization grows in size or complexity.

Because it serves as the "invisible hand" and the "connective tissue" of success, shared clarity also allows the less effective leadership model of conducting and directing to be supported by a more impactful, "purpose-centered" set of leadership behaviors focused on composing, listening, learning, modeling, teaching, coaching, and rewarding.

. . .

Shared Clarity Benefit #6:
Keeps the Fleet in Sight

Like a ship that has lost sight of the fleet, it is simply more difficult to keep everyone on the same page as they move away from the organization's center.

Without shared clarity, people tend to naturally see things through the lens of their own job or their department. Since they don't have the broader frame of reference that shared clarity provides, what they see and what they do becomes their only reality. They become disconnected or detached from what else is happening throughout the organization. This can create differing views of reality where people work to the beat to their own drum and eventually end up working at cross-purposes with other members of the organization.

The leader's core responsibility in a connected organization is to make sure that all players that have an impact on organizational success, today and in the future, clearly understand where the organization is going, how it plans to get there, and what their specific role is.

In connected organizations, leaders must find ways to have all players feel valued and know specifically how they contribute to the organization's success.

CLARITY

Keeping everyone in sight of the "fleet" is the key test of leadership in most organizations today. This can only be accomplished through an unrelenting focus on shared clarity.

• • •

Shared Clarity Benefit #7:
Makes Success Real

Bruce tells the story that almost every week, someone would call him and want to come and benchmark 3M. What they were trying to understand was the secret behind 3M's hundred-year history of innovation and growth (the secret was shared clarity).

He tells the story of some simple rules that 3M developed to reinforce their formula for success, real rules that gave people the freedom to innovate, take risks, and think outside the box.

One of these rules was the 15 percent rule. Basically it gave employees the opportunity to use 15 percent of their time to work on a project of their own choosing.

To employees it was a form of a permission slip. It gave them the opportunity to work on something that they thought could make a contribution to the company. This rule communicated very clearly that it was OK to take a risk and work on something different, and that their efforts would be appreciated by management.

The power of this rule was that it helped to connect everyone in the organization to 3M's core formula for success: innovation. It made 3M's focus on innovation real. It reinforced the shared clarity needed to help everyone translate, in a practical way, what being innovative really meant to them.

Simple and practical ideas like the 15 percent rule can help connect the organization by helping employees "live" the organization's formula for success and feel that they are part of its success.

• • •

The Value of Shared Clarity

Actions You Can Take Today

- ✔ Take a sample survey of your people to see how many of them understand your organization's formula for success strategy and their role in it.

- ✔ Ask yourself and answer the questions on page 79

- ✔ List the top three policies or procedures that may not fully support your organization's formula for success.

Section 5
Clarity Is Human

Shared clarity is defined through the hearts and minds of people. This section of the book examines the human characteristics that must be understood and dealt with for shared clarity to occur in the organization.

Clarity is Human – Introduction

Each of these human characteristics (shown below) must be considered when creating the leadership agreement and shared understanding needed to connect the organization to its formula for success.

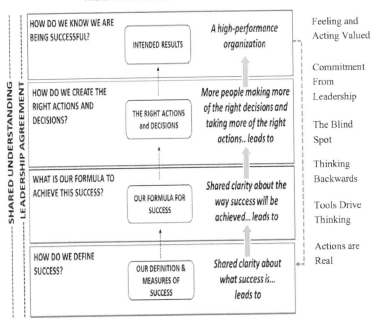

Human Characteristic #1:
Feeling and Acting Valued

We find it amazing how many organizations are managed and led on a "need to know" basis. Many employees are kept in the dark about what the overall organization is trying to accomplish. They are given guidelines, procedures, and rules to follow that apply narrowly to their jobs, roles, functions or departments. The organizational assumption is that if everyone performs his or her prescribed role well, the overall organization will be successful.

The problem with this approach is evident from the low level of "employee connectedness" found in a recent study of the US employees. This study found that:

50 percent of employees say they don't feel valued or important.

55 percent of employees are unsatisfied with their jobs.

61 percent of employees say they aren't treated with respect.

77 percent of employees say they are looking for another job.

75 percent of employees feel disengaged and not committed to their company's goals.

CLARITY

88 percent of employees say they don't get enough recognition or acknowledgement

These statistics make the upside of creating shared clarity obvious.

With shared clarity, every employee understands the actions and decisions that are important and why they are important.

Shared clarity unites and connects the organization to its members and gives everyone in the organization a broader sense of purpose and the feeling of being valuable and valued.

• • •

Human Characteristic #2:
Seeing a Commitment from Leadership

An Open Letter

    To Any Person in Our Organization:

    Like many people, every December you may head out to the mall, looking for the perfect holiday gift. You have no idea what you are looking for, but you believe you will know it when you see it. You are hoping for that moment of clarity to inspire you.

    We're sure that as a member of our team, you may have had this same feeling of uncertainty about our organization. You've probably said to yourself, "I'm not sure what they're looking for in my work, but I'm sure they will let you know when they don't see it."

    We know this leads to you to sometimes feel as if you are on a merry-go-round. Round and round it goes, where it stops, nobody knows.

    We know that you want to feel that your efforts are contributing to something that is good. We also know that the need for clarity is a part of the human spirit. It is what makes us know what's important and feel valued.

CLARITY

This letter is about our commitment to you. We promise to continually make our formula for success clear for you so you can understand your role in it and can contribute to the best of your ability.

You are valued.

Sincerely,

Organizational Leader

. . .

Human Characteristic #3:
The Blind Spot

While it is said that people will try to do the right thing, it is also true that most of what we see as "right" comes from our perceptions and is based on our personal experiences.

This creates blind spots in all of us. These blind spots are different for everyone. Because they are unique to us as individuals, blind spots present a significant challenge to creating shared clarity.

While individuals and organizations may think that they fully understand and are connected with the formula for success, they may in fact be blindly operating independently in ways that are counterproductive or even damaging to the organization.

This phenomenon is never more obvious than when we talk to executives shortly after they've participated in an off-site strategy session only to have them give us often greatly different interpretations about what was discussed and decided.

The human blind spot is a powerful force that leads to organizational disconnectedness. It can only be addressed when leaders recognize its impact as they focus on creating shared clarity.

• • •

Human Characteristic #4:
Thinking Backwards

As we have stated throughout this book, creating a connected organization requires absolute and shared clarity about the organization's current and future formula for success. This means we must have the ability to "backward translate" our personal understanding of the formula for success to the actions and decisions we make today.

As someone once said, "You read a book from front to back, from beginning to end, but you run a business just the opposite: you start with the end in mind and then work backwards to achieve it."

Rick tells the story of how the importance of thinking backwards was embedded in his mind very early in his career.

"As a young, new employee fresh out of college, I joined the finance department of a large telecommunications company. A few months after starting my career, I had the opportunity to work on a special project led by the general manager.

Upon meeting him for the first time, the GM asked me what I did for the company. I proudly said, 'I work in Finance.'

"I will never forget the GM's response when he said, 'You poor guy. Do you know what financial numbers are?'

"Being somewhat caught off guard, I said, 'Not really.'

"And then the GM said something that has stuck with me for many years: 'Financial numbers are nothing more than the net present value of past decisions. They don't just happen and they can't be changed. They were caused—they are the result of actions and decisions made a while ago.'

"After getting over my deflated sense of value, I learned a lesson that applies directly to the topic of this book: the need to think backwards."

In working with our clients, we often hear them say that this type of thinking "hurts their head." Unfortunately, the ability to think backwards is an essential human ingredient if leaders truly want to create a connected organization.

• • •

Human Characteristic #5:
Tools Drive Thinking

One of the unseen factors in organizations is how much the tools we use or don't use can drive our perspectives and our thinking.

For example, when you use Six Sigma tools, everything looks like a process. People no longer make decisions; instead they dive into the world of Six Sigma tools, processes, and teams.

When you use social media tools, people no longer talk; they text, they "Facebook," they "Link In."

When you hire an advertising agency, every solution is always advertising. When you hire a PR agency, every solution is public relations.

Tools have a direct effect on clarity in our organizations. Connected organizations must continue the search for tools that create shared clarity around and that are consistent with the organization's formula for success.

. . .

Human Characteristic #6:
Actions Are Real

The following real-life example happened to one of us about a year ago.

"Visiting a local Wal-Mart store, I spotted an employee coming down one of the aisles. She was wearing an employee badge and one of Wal-Mart's 'How Can I Help You' blue vests.

"I was looking for an electronics product, so I asked her where the electronics department was located. To my surprise, her response was, 'I'm off the clock,' and she kept moving toward the door. Since that day, I avoid shopping at Wal-Mart."

Small issue? Perhaps. Caused by a lack of shared clarity? Absolutely. Bottom line impact? Potentially big. If this happened to only 1 percent of Wal-Mart's customers, the loss in lifetime revenue would be in the hundreds of millions of dollars.

Apparently, in the case of Wal-Mart, the customer service ingredient of its formula for success was not defined or communicated explicitly or widely enough to make it clear to the manager and to this employee that this type of response to a customer was clearly not consistent with Wal-Mart's success.

Unfortunately, this example is not unique. Numerous studies have shown that many employees at all levels do not understand

and are unable to translate the organization's formula for success to what they do and how they do it. The actions these employees take and the decisions they make are real and they have a direct impact on the organization's performance. They cannot be taken back or reversed.

. . .

Clarity is Human

Actions You Can Take Today

✔ Build a version of the employee satisfaction criteria shown on pages 91-92 into your next employee survey or hold an employee focus group to discuss these issues.

✔ Write a letter or email similar to the one shown on page 93-94.

✔ Create a list of possible employee actions or decisions that could be consistent or inconsistent with your organization's formula for success. Prioritize these actions and decisions based on their relative impacts and then discuss them with your management team.

✔ Create a list of tools that could be consistent or inconsistent with your organization's formula for success. Prioritize these tools based on their relative impacts and then discuss them with your management team.

Section 6
The Future Is Now

Just like the world we live in, organizations, employees, and customers are constantly changing. This section of the book looks at the importance of achieving shared clarity in the years ahead.

The Customer of Tomorrow

Customers in the future will expect to be even more connected. They will be even more attuned to the issues that affect them. They will expect companies to make explicit promises—and to meet them.

For example, one of our three-year-old granddaughters knows how to turn on our iPad, how to unlock it, and how to select the app she wants to play with. Soon she will have her own computer, her own Facebook account, her own Twitter account, and her own LinkedIn account.

If she isn't happy with the service she receives from a business, she will be able to tell the whole world instantly through her own social network. She will also have the ability to quickly find their competitors through a myriad of Internet search engines.

More than ever before, organizations will have no choice but to be fully connected to the promise they are making to their customers. Future customers like our granddaughter will expect that promises made to them are clear and are delivered each and every time. Because they are growing up in the information age, connecting with them will not be an option.

Connecting with these future customers simply cannot happen if the organization is disconnected itself. Where there is confusion or different interpretations of what the promise of connectedness to customers means or how exactly how it will be achieved, the promise will be broken.

Ultimately the customer, especially the customer of the future—not management—will be the final judge of an organization's connectedness.

Their judgments are harsh and final.

• • •

The Employee of Tomorrow

As mentioned earlier, Bruce teaches at the University of Minnesota. His course is the last class students take before they graduate.

Needless to say, one of the big topics of conversation is careers and where students want to work.

Almost all of his students talk about wanting to find a job and have a career where they can make a difference in the world and where they can fulfill their life purpose.

They want to do something where they will feel connected. They are very clear that they do not want to work in a Dilbert-style organization. They talk openly about not wanting to work for "the man."

This is the next generation coming into the workforce. They grew up with iPods, iPads, computers, and social media. They are the connected, digital generation.

It is very clear that to attract this next generation of talent, organizations must connect their employees in meaningful ways to a higher purpose, one that goes beyond their day-to-day job.

The organization that uses clarity about its purpose and formula for success to engage and motivate its people will be the winner in the search for the next generation of talent.

• • •

The Organization of Tomorrow

Our organizations are deconstructing.

Jobs get sent overseas, jobs get outsourced, contract employees are hired, consultants are brought in, companies who specialize in particular functions get hired to replace whole departments, and companies downsize.

Fear runs rampant in our workplace. Peter Drucker even predicted the disappearance of the organization as we know it today.

This makes clarity the number-one issue in our organizations. Where are we going? What will the future look like? What's my role going forward?

The successful organization of the future will have figured out the answers to a few critical questions. What is our promise to our customers? What is our purpose? Where are we going? How do we align our organization to successfully deliver on this promise to our customers? Do our employees feel connected to the success of the organization? Do our customers feel a strong connection to our organization?

The successful organization of the future will be made up people who say, "I really feel connected to our success."

• • •

Section 7
Leading the Connected Organization

Creating shared clarity is the job of leadership. It cannot be delegated. This section of the book explores the challenges that leaders face in creating and sustaining a connected organization through shared clarity.

What the Experts Haven't Taught Us

Like us, many of you reading this book have been, are, or aspire to be, organizational leaders. Some you may study, teach, coach, or mentor current or future leaders.

There are hundreds of leadership experts out there to help us do this. These experts study the best and the worst leaders, looking for the things that define leadership greatness. They write books, hold seminars, and provide one-on-one coaching and advice. Their expertise is helpful.

What these experts haven't taught us, however, is that creating shared clarity is in many ways unnatural. As leaders, just as in people, being "too clear" can threaten our basic human desire for power, influence, and self-worth.

The experts haven't taught us that in their heart of hearts, leaders sometimes say to themselves, "I just feel more comfortable if I keep the people I have influence over a little bit in the dark. That way I can keep my options open, and I don't have to commit and put my cards on the table. I don't have to make some decisions I'm really not sure about. I feel safer."

The experts haven't taught us that great leaders overcome this basic human need for control and security. They haven't taught us that the great leaders have the confidence and courage to truly believe that their true power and influence comes not from being conductors but from being composers.

 The experts haven't taught us a fundamental truth that we have seen in the best leaders when they tell us, "I look to the organization" rather than, "The organization looks to me."

• • •

It Looks Clear From Here

In real fog, the closer things are, the clearer they become. Similarly, in the "organizational fog" created by a lack of shared clarity, it is quite natural for organizational leaders to believe that things are clear. This is because leaders have the advantage of not having to "translate" the formula for success to detailed functional actions like many others in the organization. So, while the leader thinks things are clear, the rest of the organization sees mostly fog as they try to decide what specific actions they should take or not take and what decisions they should make.

This "It's clear from here" phenomenon is supported by many studies that have repeatedly shown that while few of the organization's members understand the organization's formula for success and their specific role in it, many more organizational leaders believe things are clear.

The good news is there is a difference between real fog and organizational fog. Organizational fog can be lifted by leadership and communication.

By creating shared clarity, organizational leaders can quickly replace organizational fog with clear single vision of success.

• • •

Trust

The backbone of the connected organization is trust. In creating shared clarity, however, trust is a two-edged sword.

If leaders don't entrust employees with the "full story" about the organization's formula for success, shared clarity is impossible. Likewise, employees who feel disconnected will not always trust what they hear from leadership.

We have found that connected organizations create trust through a new type of leadership, one based on teaching, delegating, coaching, and mentoring rather than managing and controlling.

We have also found in the connected organization, leaders create trust by clearly communicating and creating understanding about why something as simple as keeping the floor clean is important to the organization's formula for success.

• • •

The Orchestra Needs a Common Score

As mentioned earlier in this book, numerous studies have shown that more than 90 percent of employees and almost half of senior executives in US companies do not fully understand the keys to their organization's success and their role in them.

This continues to be shocking to us.

This is analogous to a symphony orchestra whose musicians are each playing from a different sheet of music. Without a common musical score, each musician can only "imagine" what the symphony is supposed to sound like. Each of them plays one part to perfection, but the timing is off and the harmony is ruined.

Needless to say, the stakes are much higher for a disconnected organization than they are for a disconnected symphony orchestra. Instead of just a bad symphony, the lack of shared clarity is a recipe for greatly increased organizational, fiduciary, and personal risk. What board of directors, company, or organization would be satisfied with this level of disconnectedness in any of its other business processes?

When members of an organization are forced to "interpret" what the formula for success is and to then try to translate it into what they do and how they do it, organizational performance suffers, sometimes in a significant, non-recoverable way.

CLARITY

We believe the power of a connected organization is so great that the organization's success formula or strategy doesn't have to be perfect—that an average formula for success well executed by a connected organization will beat a great one poorly executed every time.

Shared clarity is the organization's "common musical score" for this success.

• • •

Composers First

People often get to a position of organizational leadership by being great conductors, not great composers. They rise in the organization because of their deep expertise or their ability to manage operations in an outstanding way. The skills needed to connect their organization around a clear and unifying formula for success are often not very critical to their personal success along the way.

We believe this leads to the single most critical business leadership gap in the United States today … the leader's inability to galvanize his or her team around the organization's formula for success.

Unfortunately, this critical leadership skill is not taught in business schools or corporations, nor is it often developed through on the job training or even through the "school of hard knocks."

We believe that building and sustaining a connected organization defines the ultimate destination of leadership and is embodied by the adage "The conductor may lead the orchestra, but it is the composer of the musical score and the artists who create the symphony."

· · ·

Leading the Connected Organization

Actions You Can Take Today

✔ Write down in a sentence or two your organization's definition of success. On a second piece of paper, again in a sentence or two, write down you organization's formula to achieve that success. Ask several other people you trust to do the same thing. Compare notes to see if agree and if you are "reading from the same sheet of music."

✔ Rate your abilities and performance on the critical shared clarity creating skills of teaching, delegating, coaching, and mentoring. Ask yourself, "is there any opportunity for improvement?"

Section 8
Building the Connected Organization

The key to creating shared clarity is approaching it systematically, just like any other business process. This section of the book provides a seven-step approach that you can use to create a connected organization.

Building the Connected Organization - Introduction

First and foremost, building a connected organization requires leaders who understand the importance of shared clarity to organizational performance. It also requires a systematic, process-oriented approach that employs new tools and techniques.

This section of the book provides a specific set of steps that leaders can take to create shared clarity in their organizations.

Step 1 - Approach Shared Clarity as a Process

As we said earlier, shared clarity is a process. It can and should be approached and managed just like any other process in the organization. We have addressed the components of the shared clarity process in this book and they are illustrated below.

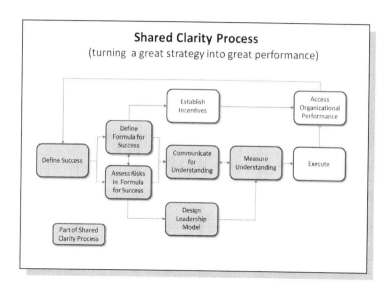

Step 2 - Walk Around Your Chair

Creating a connected organization requires leaders who think and act like the composer of a clear and common musical score.

Do this—literally: Get up, walk around your chair, and sit back down. You are now a composer rather than a conductor. If you are not comfortable with being a composer, stop here.

In your new "composer chair," ask yourself these questions:

- What are the priorities and themes of our formula for success?
- What goals does our formula for success imply, and why are they important?
- What is our approach to achieve these goals? What actions are required?
- How will we measure and communicate our success?
- What are the things we should engage our people around?
- What should I listen for?
- What should I learn?
- What behaviors should I model?
- Who and what should I teach, coach and reward?

Write down your answers to these questions. You will need them later.

Step 3 - Trust the People

Shared clarity requires trust.

The power of a connected organization comes from making things clear to all of the people, not just a few. It is about imparting knowledge to create understanding.

The leader of a connected organization must assume that people want to do the right things, regardless of their role or position. Of course, there will always be a few bad apples, but there must be a mutual level of trust that "if we all know our formula for success and our specific roles in it, we will do the right thing."

Unfortunately, we are never really surprised by the apparent lack of trust and empowerment communicated in many organizations. We've been there. The signals of low trust are often subtle, but they are nevertheless very real.

For example, what message about trust is communicated by issuing strict policies and procedures that are not accompanied with a clear explanation as to why they are important and how they fit into the organization's formula for success?

What about the often-inspiring mission and vision "signage" found on many hallway walls that are inconsistent with the "real world" that each person sees every day or that are so nebulous they are not translatable to what people actually do or how they do it?

Building the Connected Organization

What is communicated about trust when the leadership team goes off for the annual planning conference and then treats the outcome of the session as "top secret"?

To complete this step, leaders must truly believe that the organization's people can be trusted to do the right things in the right ways if they are entrusted with personalized clarity about the organization's formula for success.

Step 4 - Make Sure Your Formula for Success is Clear

As we have said throughout this book, the formula for success (even if not perfect) must be defined clearly, in sufficient detail and in ways that will help guide as many actions and decisions as possible toward success.

As such, the starting point of shared clarity must be a clear and specific formula for success—one that all members and parts of the organization will act upon in the intended ways.

Unfortunately we find that in most organizations, the formula for success is not clear or it is not shared by everyone. This fact is often immediately evident when we ask organizational leaders three simple questions: How do you define success, what is your formula to achieve it, and would others in the organization say the same thing?

We find that most leaders are able to describe their future strategy, talk about their key goals in great detail, or tell us what they accomplished in the past. However, when we ask them to boil their formula for success down to its basics, they often hesitate and say, "I haven't really thought about it that way."

We then give them a couple of real examples to help them understand what we mean.

Building the Connected Organization

For instance, we tell them about Harley Davidson, supposedly in the motorcycle business, whose formula for success is *"the design, manufacturing, sales, and distribution of nostalgia and executive jewelry."* Or about Ritz Carlton, whose formula for success is captured in the statement *"We are in the business of ladies and gentlemen serving ladies and gentlemen."*

These examples help illustrate the importance of defining the organization's "business" and its formula for its success in a way that everyone can understand and feel connected to. Only then can further clarification and communication take place.

Step 5 - Create Shared Clarity

A formula for success that can be clearly understood and translated by everyone in the organization is the foundation of a connected organization. The definition must be complete, clear, and unified. It cannot be subject to misinterpretation or "filling in the blanks."

When completing this step, leaders should always keep in mind that the next step is to communicate the formula for success to the entire organization and to gain full understanding.

We use the Shared Clarity Map as the framework for this step. This helps to make sure that the formula for success is complete, clear, and unified.

In this step, you should ask yourself the following questions about the clarity of your organization's formula for success:

IS IT COMPLETE? Does it address all relevant content? Is anything of importance assumed to be included or taken as a given?

IS IT CLEAR? Are the answers to the questions in the bottom two quadrants of the Shared Clarity Map crystal clear to each stakeholder? Are examples provided and/or are specific circumstances described to increase understanding and encourage the correct interpretation?

Building the Connected Organization

IS IT UNIFIED? Will our description of our formula for success enable us to create a common, unified interpretation and translation throughout the entire organization from top to bottom and across all functions?

Shared Clarity Map

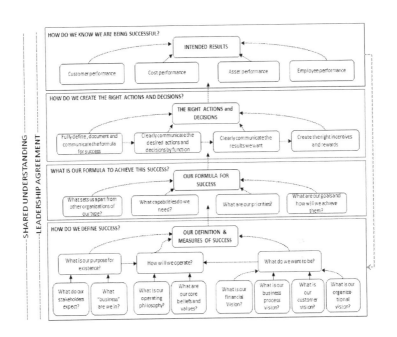

Step 6 - Create Shared Understanding

The biggest challenge in creating a connected organization is creating a clear and common understanding of the formula for success on the part of all the key stakeholders. This must be done in a way that allows each of them to personalize the "promise" of organizational success.

We have found that understanding and translation is best accomplished by structuring the communication around the following elements of the organization's formula for success:

- ✔ What are the key themes we need to focus on?
- ✔ What we are trying to achieve?
- ✔ Why these things important?
- ✔ How we will get there?
- ✔ How we will define and measure success?
- ✔ What will we need to be successful?

Step 7 - Measure Shared Clarity

As we have said throughout this book, the foundation for organizational performance is shared clarity. Therefore, just like any other key performance indicator, the degree of shared clarity can and should be measured.

Shared clarity should be measured on two dimensions: (1) organizational entity and (2) formula for success component.

Shared Clarity Measurement by Organizational Entity:

Since shared clarity is defined through the eyes of all members and levels of the organization, it must be measured the same way—by organizational level and function.

For example, it's important to know that the leadership group might score clarity high while middle managers or front line employees are unclear about some aspects of the formula for success and therefore score clarity low.

This indicates that the organization, by definition, is partially disconnected and provides valuable insights that allow leadership to better target their shared clarity efforts to the right organizational entities or levels.

Shared Clarity Measurement by Formula for Success Component:

The lack of shared clarity can also occur around certain elements of the formula for success.

For instance, there may be a high degree of shared clarity at all organization levels around the vision aspects of the formula for success but little shared clarity about the organization's business process vision.

This again indicates that the organization is disconnected—in this case around some aspects of the formula for success.

In conclusion, measuring the degree of shared clarity is an essential part of managing the organization for success and high performance. The measurement must be systematic and must address all levels of the organization and all aspects of the Shared Clarity Map.

The measurement of shared clarity must also be comprehensive and thorough.

For instance, in our work, we help our clients measure the degree of shared clarity by examining and rating more than one hundred shared clarity factors by organizational level and formula for success component.

To do this, we use our proprietary assessment tool to produce a shared clarity score we call the Connected Organization Index (COI). The COI can range between zero and one hundred.

This is often accompanied by what we call a "Connected Organization Report Card," which provides supplemental findings and recommendations (see example shown below).

Connected Organization Scorecard

SUCCESS CLARITY SCORE: 4.7		Clarity About Our Success				
		Clarity About Our Purpose	Clarity About What is Expected Of Us by Our Stakeholders	Clarity About Where We Want To Go (Our Vision)	Clarity About the Value We Provide To Our Customers	Clarity About Our Formula for Success
	Avg.	Degree to which there is perceived clarity around key strategy elements				
Organizational Level:						
LEADERSHIP	7	7	7	8	6	5
FUNCTION HEADS	6	5	7	5	6	5
MIDDLE MANAGEMENT	4	5	3	5	5	4
ADMINISTRATIVE MANAGEMENT	4	4	3	4	5	4
NON-MANAGEMENT	3	3	2	4	3	2
AVERAGE SUCCESS CLARITY SCORE	4.7	4.8	4.4	5.2	5.0	4.0
GOAL/ACTION CLARITY SCORE: 3.4		Clarity About Our Goals and Actions				
		Clarity About What We Must Accomplish	Clarity About How We Will Measure Our Accomplishments	Clarity About Our Required Actions	Clarity About How Our Systems and Processes Support Our Formula for Success	
Organizational Level:						
LEADERSHIP	6	4	5	7	6	
FUNCTION HEADS	4	4	3	5	4	
MIDDLE MANAGEMENT	3	3	3	4	3	
ADMINISTRATIVE MANAGEMENT	3	3	2	3	3	
NON-MANAGEMENT	2	3	1	2	1	
AVERAGE GOAL/ACTION CLARITY SCORE	3.4	3.2	2.8	4.2	3.4	
TOTAL CLARITY SCORE: 4.1						

However it is done, the measurement of shared clarity is an essential step in creating and maintaining a connected organization. It is also a key measure of leadership effectiveness that should be strongly weighted in the organization's management performance appraisal process.

Step 8 - Lead in the Right Way

Because organizational conditions change and new strategies are put in place, the organization's formula for success may change over time. This makes it important that organizational leaders make the preceding seven steps both a personal and organization-wide core competency that can be reapplied successfully.

Formulas for success can also vary widely by organization. Therefore, leading a connected organization calls for leadership attributes and behaviors that are specifically tailored to the formula for success. For instance, how leaders target their personal actions around recognition, rewards, coaching, and creating accountability will differ greatly under a formula for success based on product innovation versus one based on customer intimacy or low cost.

In summary, to create and sustain a connected organization, the formula for success must first be clear and then must be supported directly by the leader's behaviors and actions.

IMPROVE YOUR ORGANZATION'S PERFORMANCE STARTING TODAY

This book has been dedicated to the principle of shared clarity—that organizations more connected to their formula for success outperform. The opportunity to reap the performance benefits of improved organizational connectedness is real and immediate. We've found that organizations can increase their connectedness by 25 percent to 50 percent in thirty days or less through the three-step program described below:

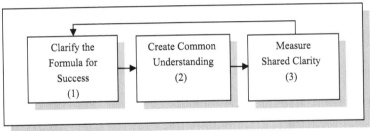

Organizational Connectedness Improvement Program

<u>Define & Clarify</u> - Leadership teams create shared clarity around their organization's formula for success through defining, exploring, debating, and reaching consensus on the foundational issues essential to achieving a connected organization.

<u>Communicate</u> - Leaders fully and clearly document the formula for success and communicate it in narrative form to the organization for personalized understanding.

<u>Measure</u> - Organization-wide measurement that quantifies the degree of shared clarity and identifies specific areas needing improvement.

Because of the direct correlation between organizational connectedness and performance, the range of performance improvement from a 25 percent improvement in the degree of shared clarity could approximate the following:

Performance Improvement Metrics:

Customer Satisfaction (+15%)

Customer Turnover (-8%)

Cost/Unit (-15%)

Employee Satisfaction (+20%)

Employee Turnover (-4%)

Gross Margin (+6%)

Return on Sales (+15%)

ROI (+6%)

OUR WORK

We believe in the extraordinary power of shared clarity.

Our work is focused on helping committed clients use the principle of shared clarity to realize higher performance and reduce organizational risk. This is our passion.

We do this by: (1) working with organizational leaders to apply the principle of shared clarity to their organizations, (2) training organizational leaders and managers in the shared clarity process, (3) developing customized curriculums that provide broad-based education on shared clarity and (4) providing tools and processes for the comprehensive measurement and benchmarking of shared clarity across organizations and industries.

SUMMARY

This book has focused on the never-ending search for shared clarity in our organizations and among people. It is about using shared clarity to unleash human potential and power team and organizational performance.

We wrote this book because the lack of shared clarity is the "elephant in the room" that is very seldom discussed or focused on by the leaders of most organizations. We find this both troublesome and amazing, but also to be a great opportunity.

The challenge to create and sustain shared clarity rests with leadership. It is a responsibility that cannot be delegated.

We hope that the lessons included in this book will help current and aspiring leaders better understand and fulfill this critical responsibility.

Rick, Bruce, and Jeff

For more information go to our website at www.yeager-group.com, contact us via email at info@yeager-group.com or call us at (772) 345-2332.

Acknowledgements

We'd also like to especially thank Mel Ray and John Gelland for their valuable insights based on their deep experience as corporate executives, entrepreneurs, leadership coaches and consultants.

About The Authors

RICHARD YEAGER - Rick is a former Fortune 50 executive and CFO. He is currently a senior management consultant who specializes in helping organizational leaders improve their organization's performance and long-term health. Rick has provided consulting services to hundreds of senior executives from more than thirty cross-industry companies worldwide.

In addition to his focus on strategic clarity, Rick has deep expertise in a number of other areas critical to organizational excellence. These include strategy, finance, activity-based management, benchmarking, change management, total quality management, performance measurement, balanced scorecard, shareholder value analysis, and business process reengineering.

BRUCE MOORHOUSE - Bruce's passion is leadership and helping organizations discover and develop their culture and identity. His thirty-year career with 3M included integrating the internal and external messages of the company around 3M's promise of innovation and helping leaders at 3M understand the behaviors that drive a culture of innovation.

Over the years, numerous companies such as Caterpillar, Ford, General Motors, and Starbucks have asked Bruce to speak or consult in their organizations on developing a culture of innovation and engaging the hearts and minds of their workers.

CLARITY

Bruce currently teaches the capstone course for undergraduates in the School of Journalism and Mass Communications at the University of Minnesota.

JEFF MESKILL - Jeff has an extensive track record in developing human systems and improving their alignment to key strategies.

Throughout his professional career, Jeff led successful integrations across a number of complex global industries and has held key international leadership positions where he challenged business units to outperform through a deep commitment of clarifying their strategic intent. This multinational experience working with different cultures, geographies, brands, and capabilities has given him deep rooted appreciation for the importance of organizations coming together and staying connected.

Bibliography

Kaplan, Robert S., and David P. Norton. 2001. *The Strategy-Focused Organization.* Boston: Harvard Business School Press

Mankins, Michael, C., and Richard Steele. 2005. *Turning Great Strategy into Great Performance:* 3

Griffin, Michael. *CFO Magazine.* November 2011.

Made in the USA
Charleston, SC
04 March 2013